My Endless
Journey

T.T. Touray

Continental
RIGHTS LLC

My Endless Journey
Copyright © 2025 by T.T. Touray

Library of Congress Control Number: 2025911593

ISBN
978-1-967804-10-8 (Paperback)
978-1-967804-11-5 (eBook)
978-1-967804-18-4 (Hardcover)

Table of Contents

Acknowledgments

Firstist and foremost, I want to thank God, my Creator, for the gift of life.

I also extend my deepest gratitude and love to my incredible family—starting with my parents, especially my mother, my "Mama Africa," who has been my rock. To my siblings—Fatimah, Aisha, Sainny, Alio, Ousman, and Abdoulie—and to my beloved brother Babacar (ROBZ) Touray, whose life was a gift and whose passing in 2020 left a deep void. May he continue to rest in peace.

To my amazing nieces and nephew—Princess, F.E., V. Boy, Little Mama, and Sain—thank you for the love, joy, and encouragement you brought into my life every single day. And to the rest of my extended family, both here and in Africa, thank you for your unwavering support, blessings, wisdom, and empowerment throughout my life.

I would also like to express special thanks to those who have made a significant impact on my journey, beginning with my Bartlett High School family. A heartfelt thank-you to the extraordinary women who became like second mothers to me: Ms. Lori King, Mrs. Wanda Galloway Ross, and the late Tanya Taylor—may she continue to rest in peace. I'm also grateful to Mr. Ray Johnson, my high school guidance counselor, and to close friends Juliette Rosado (Juju), Princess Vicent, and Balogun Bishop, as well as other dear friends like Shinoh Chung.

To my incredible team, whom I proudly call my second family—thank you for your dedication and support. I am truly honored to be part of such a remarkable group.

A special shout-out to the hardworking, passionate individuals I've had the privilege to work with—especially my Cady House family. You have not only been teammates but also like family to me.

Finally, I want to give a heartfelt thank-you to my phenomenal team at Continental Right—starting with my agent, Angel Lopez, and Zee, along with the rest of the amazing team. Your exceptional work, dedication, and collaboration helped bring this book to life.

Thank you all, from the bottom of my heart. May God bless each and every one of you.

Chapter 1

My Life Journal from West Africa to the United States

My family and I took a long journey from West Africa, a land that welcome everyone no matter who you are and where you came from, a continent full of many different African Dialogue languages, traditions, cultures, music, dances styles, more food recipes than anywhere in the world and the wonderful spirit of the African people. African homeland, I'm very blessed to be African, my faith, my African roots and values taught me many valuable lessons that become my guiding force in my life. I came a long way and overcome many obstacles in my life because of my God, my faith, the lessons and tools my parents and family taught me since, it provide me with the different tools, I needed to survive any challenges and obstacle I'm face with.

The knowledge I gained from personal experiences and my family over the years it both guided me through many aspects of my life and also provided me with some essential wisdom in my life. I'm very fortunate to have experienced the good, bad, and the worst. Seeing the suffering my African people go through daily basis due to poverty, diseases, natural disasters breaks my heart.

In every aspect of my life, I consider myself lucky to have the life, and compared to billions of African people and others

1

around the world who are suffering every day and fighting for survival. I can said that I'm thankful for the experiences I have every day. The dangers, horrors, bad and sad things we see, hear, and read about every day gave me a different perspective on life, especially what my fellow African people go through.

It's tough for anyone to see—the lack of primary living resources, foods to eat, clean drinking water, having good and warm clothing to wear, not having shelters to live in, or having the opportunities to attend a school like my siblings and I did. Those are the hardest things I must see and deal with because the people that I love and care about are going through the hardest things in life.

I feel hopeless and helpless, and it's very hard for me because I try to make a difference in my fellow African people's lives, but no matter how much I try, I never get close to helping them. I will never give up until the day I die. Even though every day I feel helpless, powerless, and useless to make a difference to both African children and adults to find a cure for the sick and dying children and help adults in need not only in Africa. But also around the world, because I'm very hurt and heartbroken to hear and see every single day what is going on in the world. A large number of people are dying, both children and adults, and not only in Africa.

I want to decrease those large numbers due to poverty, wars, diseases, etc. I want to give those people something to hold on to and look forward to because most of those things are caused by poverty. It's some things that I have been through, seen also have experienced many more of that through my African people's lives. Those experiences remind me of every waking moment of my life, and it makes me work even harder each day so that I can achieve the passion I have for my African people and others someday to have the chance to put those passions into play and those experiences and memories that I had to make a difference. Those are things that will stay with me for the rest of my life.

It makes me want to work very hard every day of my life and dream it every day so that someday I will be able to be free and end-all of those people's suffering around the world. It's a promise I make to myself that eventually, I will make a difference in African people's and also others' lives because I have this desire. I promised myself I would make a difference in others' lives someday. My friends tend to think I'm crazy or I'm losing my mind, but I take my mission and goals very seriously because of my passion and dreams.

Not everyone will understand, but for me, it's one of the essential things in my life and very special. It is personal and is something I've wanted to do since I was little. I didn't get the chance to do it until now. Those experiences that I had in Africa are things money can't buy.

In April of 2006, my father brought my sister and me to the U.S to have the American dream and to have different opportunities like a good education and other resources that were not available to me back in Africa. I got to experience the wonderful life the United States has to offer. I wish someday I can also give other people the opportunities that the U.S. has given me and also to share it with others around the world. I also want to use those experiences and skills to help turn my African people's lives and free them from poverty and end their suffering.

I know now why people call it the American dream because America is a land that opens different opportunities for people of different colors and different races for a better future and hope for tomorrow. America is a land of freedom that helps people to believe that they can achieve whatever dreams or goals they might have and want in life and their passion are and also to help them follow and achieve their American dreams and goals that we have with different opportunities for better lives for tomorrow. Also, America is a land of honor and courage. I see the encouragement in every American eye.

My family and I are very thankful to be here in the United States today, to follow the American dreams and goals we each have in our lives. Our American dream started here in Alaska, one of the largest, coldest, and snowiest states in the United States. Also in the summer, it is still cold, and there is little sunshine. While in the wintertime it gets very cold and snows almost every day but that doesn't stop people from enjoying the beautiful things and the wonderful outdoor activities Alaska has to offer.

There is one thing that I love about living in Alaska. It is a peaceful place and a great state to live in because Alaska is a place where you can focus on school, get a good job, and be yourself. You can be the person you want to be without being surrounded by drama or trouble. How I can describe the feeling of my new home is that Alaska has blessed me with so many incredible people, from my friends to teachers, coaches, and others. I have so much to be thankful for. I don't know where my American dreams will take me tomorrow; only God knows. But I know one thing for sure—God is great in so many ways, and wherever life takes me tomorrow, I will always be thankful. At the same time, the fun thing about living in Alaska is that there is a lot of activities and beautiful stuff to experience from mountain climbing to snow racing.

I was very blessed to be living in Alaska, the most magnificent land. I love my family and friends. I am following my American dream with the love and support of wonderful parents, sisters, brothers, grandparents, uncles, aunts, and the rest of my families and friends back in Africa and here in the United States.

Most of the time when my friends from other states and Europe ask me what state I do like to live in if I got the chance my answer always is Alaska. Also, the funny thing about it is that living in Alaska has blessed me with wonderful things, but my friends ask me why I still want to live in Alaska because it is cold. They would never understand the reason I chose Alaska above other states. I get asked one question over and over again about where Alaska is and why Alaska is the coldest state. Because of Alaska's weather, others tend to think Alaska doesn't have all the fun things other states have, but that is not the case.

Alaska is an enjoyable state too and has so much to offer, not only the freezing weather, or snow. Others don't realize that Alaska is a fantastic, fun, and beautiful state. I tend to tell my friends, "Don't believe what others say about Alaska until you live or visit there." People tend to think that I'm supporting Alaska because I live there, but that is not the case at all.

Because people tend to go by what others say about a place or thing before they experience it, I come across so many people upstate who want to visit Alaska but are afraid of the cold Alaskan weather. I tell people about the fact that Alaska is unique in its ways and is different from many states in the U.S. and the world. I can say for sure in many aspects I consider myself very fortunate to be able to experience so many beautiful things Alaska has to offer because I live there with my family and also did my high school and college there. I have lived the American dream as well as what Alaska has to offer in so many ways such as PFDs, money Alaskan people get, good housing opportunities for low-income families, excellent job positions, food assistance, childcare assistance, and many more.

I'm very thankful to be here in the United States today with my family and friends. My family and I took a long journey to come here to the United States to come to live in our American dream. That pride we have for the American dream shows in our eyes. I'm thrilled to be part of the fantastic things the American dream has to offer and those are the feelings that show me the impact the American dream has made in people's lives. Those are the things that the American dream has taught me and is still teaching me different opportunities and experiences that I didn't know before.

Each day is a new lesson for me, and I have so much to learn about what the American dreams have to offer and what my American dream holds for my family and me tomorrow. It's the best gift that America has provided to so many people who come to the U.S. for better lives and different opportunities. I love and have so much joy hearing my sisters telling me the new things they learn every single day in school and the fun activities they did and seeing how much they appreciate school. Living the American dream touches people in so many ways.

Every day I hear people talk about what America has blessed them with—those happy memories—and to listen to my sisters talk about the importance of families. I love being around children because you get to learn so much from children and adults. The reason why I'm here today is because of my amazing family who stood by me along the way through the experience and encouraging journey from West Africa to the United States of America.

I love being around children because I get to learn different things from children and know what their passion is and because children are the best ones to prove the impact of the American dream. In adults, you couldn't see it or learn much from them.

Those beautiful smiles on their face—are the smiles of joy and happiness that the American dream brought to people's lives.

However there is nothing more fun and exciting than seeing the awesome smiles on everyone's face and the long journey we all took from our homeland, our father's and mother's land, to come to the U.S. to follow our American dreams, our destiny, and our passions.

It's especially true when I look at my litter sister, Sainny, 7, hearing her share her likes, dislikes, and the passion she has for the future, what she wants to do by traveling all over the world or becoming a doctor. She thinks that doctors are fantastic and they give fun things to children such as treats and make sure they're doing well and fine. My two little brothers, Ousman, Abdoulie, and Alio, have different passions about what they want to be. Alio said he wants to become a firefighter and Ousman said he wants to become a doctor, Abdou want to be chef. Those kinds of passion I saw in their eyes are the reason we all came to the United States to follow our American dreams. Those are the reason we do what we do every day of our lives. It gives us the hope and courage we each have and the long journey we each take from where we each came from and what makes us unique. That is what makes us strong and independent individuals, by sticking together as one person and one big family.

It's the things that keep us going and help us dream big. We never let our fear or emotion hold us back from who we are and what we set out to do in life. We work extremely hard and try to do something better with our lives and don't let anything hold us back from being the best we can be, doing all the great things we were born to do. We need our families to help us do and get there.

I'm over blessed and grateful to have my incredible family in my life to get through so many hardships together and overcome a lot of walls and blocks that not many people can get through. We came a long way and had so many ups, downs, and challenges in life that we have faced and continue to suffer in our individual personal lives. God has always been good to us in so many ways and never gave upon us. My family and I have traveled from Africa to come to the U.S. to follow our American dreams and the passion we all have made it all worthwhile. We each have individual goals that we want to achieve in life. I know that someday God will bless me with the opportunity to make a difference all over the world. He answers all prayers. He has something in store for me in the future because of the belief and the faith I have in myself and the promise I made to God that one day I will stand up for others who can't stand up for themselves and give voice to others all over the world.

There were so many times I wish could do things differently, but sometimes things don't go the way I plan them to go. That is how life works; those are the things that make me want to work harder, and it shows me what I need to do differently so that next time I can learn from my mistakes. It taught me that life is a lesson to learn because it's full of mistakes. The important thing is to know how to learn from those mistakes and move on.

My family and I went through the hardest things in life that no one should go through and along the way, we overcame those challenges to get to where we are now. It wasn't easy, but we passed it with the strength, courage, love, and support God has blessed us. We had to work extremely hard every single day to overcome and get through the many challenges and darkness we each have in our personal lives and all the sacrifices my parents had to make for us to come to the United States. It was the price my parents paid for us to get better lives so that someday we can also give others better lives too and help our families that suffer.

My parents taught me to make them proud and continue to challenge myself in everything I do and also to achieve so many successes and accomplishments in my lifetime. I challenged myself in everything I do every single day of my life so that someday I would be able to make a difference in others' lives like my parents and family did to keep their leagues going. Because my family is the reason why I'm here in the U.S. today, it caused significant problems in our family and caused our family to break up and fall apart because not everyone in my family got to live better lives and have an education.

After we came to the U.S., there was a lot of drama back home in Africa, driving our family to the point of breaking up and dividing. From there, everything fell apart because of hurt feelings, selfishness, and jealousy of half of my family to split our happy family. Ungratefulness caused family problems, and many issues affected our family in so many ways we didn't even see it coming. What kills me inside is that those people who divided our family are the family members that my parents sacrificed so much for, from paying for the best education possible to getting valuable jobs. When I think about all of that, it hurt me a lot and broke my heart to know that those are the people who broke our happy family apart for their selfishness and selfish and wicked reasons.

Sometimes when I think about the way, our family was happy, and know-how our family is, it's all of that success. That affected my life, and every day I pray to God to bring happiness and joy to my family to gain back what we lose and what my family and I use to have before everything was lost. I will never stop believing and hoping that one day God will answer my prayers. My prayer will come true, and everyone will come together as one people and one big family and forget about the past and our differences so that we can get that cool, fun, and happy family we used to be and get my family back in one piece. That is my wish and prayed to God every morning when I wake up.

I have so much to be thankful to both of my parents. Both of my parents put their lives on hold for us. I have seen and experienced everything my parents and family taught me and the fight for us to get a better life in so many ways so that our children and grandchildren can have a better life as well. Also someday I can use those opportunities, courage, strength, and hope my American dream has blessed me enough to help my African people and others around the world. I had to learn things in hard ways about life; that was how I was raised. Some aspect still stays with me to this day, and the challenges and the many sacrifices along the way bring us together and make us stronger.

Those journeys my family, and I took from the Gambia in West Africa to come to the United States to find our destiny here helped me to learn, acknowledge, and know a lot of things in life that I didn't know before. The journey was worth it because it's my first dream to come true for me and it gives me strength and encouragement that I can do anything I put my mind to in life.

However, sometimes I think about Africa and remember all the fun and joyful things my family, friends, and I used to do before I came to the U.S. All those fun memories of Africa that I still remember are just like yesterday—the events, traditions, even the dances, musicals styles, etc. I have missed and left them behind to come to the U.S to follow my dreams, goals, and passion, but also for a better life. Those fun memories I had in my homeland are the memories that make me who

I am, and I should work extremely hard so that someday I can make changes in my homeland to make it better for my African people.

I'm fortunate and blessed to have some things others can only dream about, to have my both parents and my family members who gave up so much. So many people dream of coming to America to get a better life. For my family and me to be in the U.S. today is a big blessing and the best gift of life.

My family and I have been seeing many sides of life. It has taught me to use those experiences and turn them into something useful and better for both myself and others around the world. We have each other's back, and when one of us falls, we all fall together as a family. Also, that is what gave me the strength to keep going even after all the challenges I still face in my everyday life. Most young people my age or older don't go through something like that, but I never lost faith. It's because I have my family by my side helping me get through things.

I don't tell anyone, even my close friends, about what I go through because it is my secret. I always pretend to everyone that I'm good and everything is okay in my life because I don't share those personal things with anyone. If people knew what I have to go through every day of my life, they wouldn't say my life is perfect. I don't want to disturb people with my problems, and that is the thing my family and I must deal with and fight to work hard every day of my life. That is my personal life and my family secret which is something that I don't like to talk about with others.

Growing up in both Gambia and Alaska, I have learned a valuable lesson about so many things and that if you want something in life you have to fight hard for it. Never let opportunities pass you. You must go and find it first. Whatever you do in life, you should work hard and challenge yourself and achieve hard things that look like they can't do. The lessons my parents taught me will guard me in my future and what tomorrow holds for me because those are the things that money or fame can't fix. It's the encouragement that my parents, family, and others taught me.

I still remember the day my big sister and I came to the U.S when we first landed in LaGuardia NY. That feeling I had in a hurry to reunite with my mother and baby sister who we never saw in person before that join was one of the memorable moments in my life cause it was a mixed moment of both joy and sadness reunited with our mom. Before that, we were greeted by our uncle at the airport in the bagging clam we can pick us up from the airport and took us to his house where our mom and little sister were, after a couple of minute's drives from the airport to our uncle's house. We finally reach his place; my mom was standing outside with family waiting for us, that feeling of seeing our mom for the first time in a long time. As well with our baby sister for the first time was a moment that either my sister or I would ever forget that moment, even though I was young at the time when she left, I could still remember my mother's face and smile.

The day we arrived in NY it was the beginning of the summer it was imposing because during that time the weather was very friendly which reminded me of the African moment. The next day, my mom took us outside to show us around. I asked my mom why the Bronx apartment buildings were so tall and the rooms so small. My mom laughed then. Even though it en a very long time, most people would forget something like this, but for some reason, it still stuck in my mind hearing my mother saying "because New York had so many people, but Alaska was very different. Then she continues saying "Alaska apartments are like a house and huge. "Then she said to us "You guys will like it there because Alaska is a nice place to live." That was the first time my sister, and I even knew where Alaska was.

During those two weeks, we were in New York, and I learned why people called it the big apple. Those two weeks I discovered the New York City lifestyle and the different colors of people who lived in New York, and so many African people lived there. They had businesses there as well, and I learned that NYC is a wonderful place for vacations and holidays but is not a place for me to live. It's costly to live there because there are so many people in NYC and there are so many people who want to live there. Also gain a better understanding of why people call New York a big apple because of its diversity, different cultural festivals the city hold so many fun and cool things to do in NYC also the city that welcome everybody and make everyone feel at home, big new york family regardless of your ethnicities, race, and gender, religion. Being in NY, I have learned and discovered many valuable lessons; one of them was you can never get bored in New York City because there are many different things to do there. Everywhere you go in New York City, people are having fun and good times, and children are playing together and enjoying their childhood. Both young people and adults hang out have fun. Those are what make New York City fun and wonderful at the same time. Also, many diverse community groups can freely practice their faith belief without being discriminated against. There is also a sizeable African community there especially around Bronx areas with their different businesses. To also discover that majority eve, not all immigrants who came to NY all brought their own cultures and tradition with them to New York City that's to add to NY culture that's why make NY unique and great in all aspects.

After two months in NY, we took a flight to Alaska with our mom and baby sister where both of our parents resided.

One thing I noticed when we were going to Alaska is that to get to Alaska; there is more than one change flight to take to get there because there's no direct flight between NY to Alaska. You must change the flight to Seattle mostly then take another flight to Alaska, which overall is a long flight journey because Alaska is so far. In our case, we came through Seattle-Tacoma International Airport and took an Alaska Airline. To Alaska According to my mom, we left NY at 6 am and arrived in Anchorage Alaska International Airport around 12 afternoons, to me that was my second longest travel flight after the eight hours plus from Africa to NY. I received my very first experience of Alaska weather outside of the airport when we arrived and the funny part about it was it was summertime, and it was cold, wintry weather that I never felt before. When I decided to reflect on our journey from NY to Alaska with my mom's help, helped me recall so many things that happened, for instance the first question I asked her outside of the Anchorage airport about the chilly weather we were experiencing at the time. "Why is cold in the summertime?" Then she told us New York and Alaska were very different. It snows a lot, and that is why many people don't like Alaska. But Alaska is a wonderful place to live in, and we would like it when we got used to it. After we got our stuff, we stepped outside to take a cab and go to our house. It was freezing out. My sister and I almost froze to death even though we had two to three coats on. We were not used to that kind of weather.

My mom and baby sister looked like they were not feeling the cold because they were used to it. It doesn't get cold like that in most of Africa. The weather is very hot, so my sister and I were not used to it. After we arrived inside the house, I didn't even want to take my jackets off because at that moment we were freezing. Then after we ate and got some rest, my mom tried to take us to explore the city that day, but it didn't work out. I remember my sister and me telling our mom we didn't want to die cause was cold outside, and we didn't want to go through the cold.

I remember when my aunts and uncles came to visit us, they welcomed us to Alaska and asked how we liked it so far. Every time we told them about our Alaska experience from the airport to home, they laughed but then told us we wouldn't feel the cold when we get used to it. I remember saying I didn't want to get used to it. I wanted to go back to Africa. The following day, my mom took us out to see and explore the city and to get familiar with the town. It was beautiful, but it was cold.

We went to Anchorage malls and other places. We were outside for about two hours when I told my mom I wanted to go home because it was freezing out. Then we went home even though she wanted to show us so many places around the city that day. I learned that day Alaska is not like New York in so many ways because Alaska is cool, not crowded, and a peaceful place where you can focus on so many things and is not like the city.

It was a significant difference for my sister and me because, in Gambia, West Africa, it's sweltering and rainy throughout the year. There are also traditions and cultural events that happen throughout the year, and in the summer, it attracts many Black Americans through their need to make connections to their past. Africa is a land of history and languages that educated people about the meaning of cultures, traditions, and different styles. I miss all the fun things I used to do with my family. In a way, New York City reminded me of Africa. That's the way African people live. There is more to life and many places to see. I believe you don't know what is out there until you go out in the world. I used to think I saw everything this world had

15

to offer in Africa until I came here to the U.S. I learned that there is more to life than we think. Alaska was a significant transformation for my sister and me in so many ways such as seeing the snow for the first time when we arrived in Anchorage.

Reflecting on my experience of my beginning days in Alaska from the weather to the life it was and still, an amazing experience both good and bad. Looking back on my very first day of school in Alaska to my long through to graduating high school in Alaska how far I have come and the challenges I have to overcome. Starting with the first day of school in Alaska at the beginning wasn't easy honestly speaking, I had to face many obstacles and stuffer, but the help of my family and amazing friends, teachers, and others help make my journey more comfortable. Especially High School is a different story itself; we all who were there, and experienced high school have our own stories about it. So, this is part of my story about high school. I went to Bartlett High school in Anchorage, Alaska, (home of the golden bears). I still recall some details about my fit day of school was scary, many mixed feeling about it, the same time trying to fit in like the rest of the students also with the different challenges it brings a lot like making new friends, starting a new learning environment, I felt so many things could go wrong. But it did not go like that. My first day of school was cool because everyone was super nice, friendly, and they made me feel welcome. When I went to the main office to get my school schedule, all the staff were amicable and welcoming.

After they helped me get my school schedule, I got lost because it was very confusing for me. But other students and teachers in the hall helped me to find my way to my classes, and when I went to my classes, all my teachers were cool, friendly, and welcoming. Even though it has been so long but I still have some memories of the first day I met so many friends in all my classes, and I was fortunate to meet so many nice teachers. From that day, those nice teachers and the students I became friends with became my second families such as Ms. Taylor, Mrs. Rouse, Ms. King, Mr. Johnson, Juju, Princess, and many more. I'm very grateful to all my Bartlett friends for their warm welcome, kindness, and for making me feel like the rest of the students. Thanks to God, my fantastic family's love, support, and to all my Bartlett teachers, friends, and staff who helped me throughout my time being there from homework, school assignments, studying, preparing for college, and many other things.

Everything I have learns from kindergarten through middle school didn't even compare to my high school experience in terms of the environment that every student is trying for themselves to help them survive the four years of high school not only in the academy but in general aspect. I can say I was one of the lucky ones who avoided the high school drama and everything it came along with for the most part during my high school years because of my creditable best friends, teachers, coaches/mentors. They each helped me a lot also help me put all my focus on my academy and sports to avoid mixing with the wrong crowds. Which helped me survive my high school years also help prepare me for some level of the world of high school. Everyone who attends high school in the U.S knew how high school could be and we each have our own experience about H.S it is where students trying to both find themselves or other cases rebrand themselves to be somebody who can fit in with the rest of the popular students and crowds. It's now funny to even think about the past during my high school years was also another time I didn't forget because I spend any parts of my youth in school in the sports field. I was barely at home between school, after-school tutoring sessions, and my sports practice took over my life. I hardly didn't have what others might call fun or normal teenage life, my seven dathe ys of the week shared between my academic and sport no social life or teen life for that matter. Its always about focusing on those two important things at the same time trying to survive being a teenager in high school make it twice hard but with the help of all my family, best friends, teachers, coaches/mention help I get to where I needed to be and finally made it and graduated May 11, 2010, with my class. With the unconditional love, support, and help of my family, my teachers, friends, and guardian angel Mr. Johnson and many more. Who helped me so many ways to be on the right track to graduate with my friends. Then I follow the next chapter of my life was to attend the University of Alaska Anchorage (UAA) also getting help paying for my school.

During my senior year before I graduated from Bartlett High School, I got a summer job at J.C. Penney where my dad and my sister were working at the time as customer service assistants. I was working there until the summer's end. I returned to school to get ready for graduation. Before I graduated, I won so many academic achievement awards, sports awards, scholarships to division one teams to play sports, and community service awards including presidential volunteer service awards from President Obama. All thanks to my inspiring families for the love, support, and sacrifice they have made for me. I'm very grateful for having a strong, cool mom, dad, big sister, and the rest of my sweet family and to all my creditable teachers and friends for the kindness and support they all have given me.

After graduation, I started work. Then I started school that falls at the University of Alaska Anchorage (UAA). I had six different scholarships to attend division one schools for track & field and soccer, but I decided to take one semester at UAA then choose one of those division one schools to attend. But after one semester at UAA, I decided to stay for another one in Anchorage because I was dealing with personal issues in my life that I needed to deal with before leaving Alaska.

But after two semesters in Alaska, I decided to give up sports for personal reasons. I know others will think that is crazy for having that opportunity and giving it up. I gave up those scholarships for something that I believe in, and I stand up for what I believe in to try to make difference and try new things such as work training programs and leadership programs. My school schedule was hectic. No days off for me. I worked and even went to school full-time. I worked hard to get good grades. I tried hard to be a good student and person and make my family proud. There was no way I would allow anything to hold me back from getting or achieving anything I wanted in life. I know I can do anything and even achieve impossible things.

I know that life is full of secrets and mysteries and the essential part of all is how to keep those secrets safe. I think that some things about us should keep to ourselves. The funny thing is I always try my best to do the right things, but sometimes things don't go the way I planned, but at the end of the day, God shows me the right path.

I always dream about making a significant difference in people's lives all over the world. To make that dream come true, I need higher education and to work hard. Life is not as hard as we think it is we must know how to take the right steps. Nothing is easy or free in life. Also up to you to make it, and sometimes my friends think I'm crazy because I don't get any breaks or rest. I take every day as a challenge. I believe that whatever you do in life, you should always give it 100% because everyone has people counting on them. That is why we should be good role models, not only for our families and friends but also for our communities and the future leaders of tomorrow.

Life is too short, and we each want to make an example and memories that people can remember us.

I'm fortunate to have good people in my life to guide me throughout my whole life—my awesome parents, big sister, other family members, my close friends, my coaches, officers, teammates, teachers, and many more. Also, God has blessed me with amazing people in my life that I'm thankful for that because not a lot of people have that kind of blessing.

That is why people like me who are lucky to have that kind of gift from God reminded me to use those tools and experiences to help my fellow African people, to be able to have better lives and better futures. I never give up hope that one day their dreams will come true. I know that I have what it takes to make those dreams happen if I take chances and work hard.

Before, the way I dealt with stress was by doing sports and running. It made me feel better. But now, after my near-death experience with a brain tumor, I developed a new talent that I never knew I had before. It is my calling of writing. Now I deal with complicated stuff by writing. That is what makes me feel better. As well it made me feel good about myself, and it showed me a path through which everything would be okay, and I would recover from the tumor. I will be myself again.

It helped me find my voice and to use this new ability to be the voice of others. Writing helps me to deal with my issues and to free my mind. It helps me to explore my feelings and the things that I don't talk about through my writing. I can express those feelings I don't like to talk about It in general. During my recovery process, I used to hate it when my doctor said those words to me. It is going to take time before your brain gets back to normal. But I know one thing for sure—I have a second chance at life to make a difference in the world.

It kills me inside not to be able to express those feelings and talk about some things like seeing my mom most of the time walk to work and back home because when she got off from work, the bus service closed. She didn't want to use her tips to take cabs. She tried to use them to buy things in the house to support the family. She worked to put food on the table for us and pay the bills with the help of my big sister who also worked day and night with no days off. My dad has also been the best even though things are not the way they used to be.

It breaks my heart to see my mom must go through all that and must sacrifice everything for us. I wish I could help take some responsibilities from them. I was so sick I couldn't even walk home from the hospital to finish recovering at home. Seeing them go through that held my recovery back several times because I kept everything inside of me. I remember my doctor telling me all the time that my stress level is exceedingly high and that's not good for me during those times. It can take all my processes backward, and it can make my condition worse.

Looking back, I'm very thankful to get back to myself again, and now I can help with some of the responsibilities. For the first time, all those feelings I kept inside of me can be shared with the world so that my experience can help others too.

I felt like there was not tomorrow for me during those times because I couldn't even help myself or my mom. I felt like I was going to die, but my mom, sister, and family stood by me, helping me to get well. There is nothing good enough to pay them for their sacrifices. I didn't think there was a second chance in life for me, but they held me together. I'm tumor-free today Feb 12, 2013, and for all the sacrifices my family made for me I'm forever thankful.

Throughout my life, I have experienced and seen so many times my parents and sister have put their lives and dreams on hold countless times for our family. It hurts me so much to think about everything my parents had to give up for us, even their dreams, and see my big sister do the same thing. I'm very blessed to have such parents and a big sister like that. There were so many challenges and tough times we overcame together as a family, but God always showed us the way to pass those difficulties. That is what life is all about; you have good and tough times but what matters is how to get through those tough times.

The funny thing about it is that people see me smiling and they think my life is perfect and great and others keep telling me they wish they had my life. But what they didn't know the things I have overcome. They don't see what is behind the mask of smiles.

I know that putting smiles on my face and not facing my fears and nightmares is not the right thing to deal with those personal issues. Keeping everything inside can cause more problems with my health, and that's what happened to me when I become diagnosed with a brain tumor it also brings many problems along to me from dealing with my worst nightmare, and my other nightmares added to my problems. Everything I kept inside for a long time almost killed me.

Every day is a lesson for me because I get to learn new things about life. Being here in the U.S. also makes me realize that life is so much more than what I thought it was. It has opened my mind about a lot of things such as new things, skills, and other experiences to add to ones I had and opens my eyes more than I can ever imagine and help me to view things differently and to see things in other people's point of view.

It's apparent to me now and has a better understanding that God has a plan for me in the future, and there is a reason why I'm here in the U.S. today and doing the best I can to live in the American dream. Through my journey here, I also learned that everything happens for a reason. Sometimes some problematic things and challenges we face in our lives are signs from God to show us the path to our destiny and the valuable lesson I learned is that every day is a new day, but if we don't learn from those mistakes, we will make the same mistakes over again.

Now the important lesson I learned during my recovery from a brain tumor is that some of the people I thought were my family and close friends weren't they were people taking advantage of my family and me also It took me so long to see it. Also being diagnosed with a brain tumor was one of the best things ever to happen to me because it made me discover so much about myself that I didn't know before. What makes me mad and disappointed is other people taking advantage of my mom and sister. If it were just me, I wouldn't have been bothered.

I don't like people who are ungrateful to others who gave up everything to give them better lives. I have seen that firsthand because I have seen my parents, sister, and myself go through that several times. Because of all the things I have been through now I have a problem trusting people or even opening to people about my feelings and the things that I'm dealing with in my personal life. I also hate people lying to me, pretending like they care when they don't; they just needed something from me.

Now my life is not back to normal, even though I'm tumor-free. Sometimes it makes me go crazy because I want to get back to normal now. It has been a long time being sick, not been able to do anything for myself. Those were very dark times in my adult life, not knowing if I'm going to die or survive. Besides all the challenges and challenging times in my life, trying to finish my last recovery, I also had to overcome my fear and try to deal with the issues in my life. I'm dealing with everything step by step and having faith in God and believing in myself.

During my journey, I learned that truth is a significant issue in so many people's lives. After everything I have been through, sometimes I have trust issues because so many people betrayed me. I know I should let people care about it because you get to live in this life once. If you don't live it and learn to trust people, you can't get those times back; it's gone forever.

Chapter 2

My passion for better lives for the African people

I love helping people, and my passion is someday to make a difference in others' lives. My mission is an attempt to stand up for others who can't stand for themselves and to help others like my mom and big sister. My passion for helping others started when I was a little girl and my desire to help came from both my parents, big sister, grandparents, and other family members. Their love and generosity to people made me want to do the best I could to be like them to make a difference.

They all taught me something. If you open your heart to people and help people, good things will come to you. Also, I enjoy working with different people because I get to learn more things from them. I love volunteering with different people and foundations to help people in the community. The love and desire I had for helping people inspired me to start my website foundation to let people know the different organizations their people can donate to, helping others in need. Hopefully, someday I can begin my foundation across the globe. I have come so far to make a difference in people's lives. I even created a website called the HTIN 2010 Foundation to help people in any way possible to make sure children out there are fed and have their basic needs met.

Hopefully, someday, the HTIN 2010 will make a significant impact and help people in Africa who are suffering from HIV/AIDS and other diseases and one day open different opportunities for people in need all over the world. In most of the world, children in demand lack education, including in Africa. I believe that someday the passion I have for my dream foundation will make a difference and provide people with basic needs. I know that nothing comes easy, and I must work hard to get to where I'm going in life. I believe in taking every day as a challenge to make my passion come true for the love of making a difference in people's lives.

There are more than 2.1 billion people around the world who are suffering, and they need help so seriously. To see the sadness and fears in their eyes, I wish every night when I go to sleep that when I wake up in the morning, there will be good news for me about making my foundation dream come true. With all my disappointment, I never lost hope because the promise I made to myself is that no matter what, I would never give up on my dreams and passions. I will try to do whatever it takes to make a difference in people's lives.

Generally, I want my foundation to improve health standards and education for people in need. It is to create hope for the hopeless, homes for the homeless, and education for the illiterate. It also aims to ensure these innocents live in healthy conditions and enjoy what other humans who are in better lives enjoy.

I realize that to help African people orphaned because of AIDS and other diseases, the people in the region must be protected from poverty, abysmal ignorance, wars, and malnutrition. The people (men, women, and children as well as elderly) must have quality education, an adequate balanced diet, safe drinking water, and good health care delivery systems.

This is the way to combat AIDS and subsequently reduce the number of orphans. Even though a little virus causes AIDS, the challenge it imposes on humanity is beyond the boundary of the most sophisticated laboratory in the world. It is heartbreaking that our African people are going through this, and I wish that one day my passion for my foundation can make a difference.

The majority of the world's children who are orphaned by HIV/AIDS and other diseases live in Africa. These children live mostly in environments where chronic malnutrition, abject poverty, destitution, violence, and sexual abuse are widespread. I believe and think that someday my foundation will make a difference in people's lives. Innocent children are vulnerable as they are not in any way responsible for these tragedies.

When I think about those helpless children and their families, it is painful. They are not in any position to maintain personal hygiene. In some circumstances, they even lack safe drinking water. As a result, infectious diseases like cholera, scabies, and diarrheal diseases emerge among these people because of the poor conditions. Most of these infectious diseases are very deadly and life-threatening without immediate detection and diagnosis.

Furthermore, for intervention strategies to be effective and sustainable, the communities and people concerned must outline their specific needs, problems, and how to mitigate the prevailing challenges. A comprehensive plan will also be developed that would aim at integrating these children into society so that they feel like the rest of the children. Advocacy as well as sensitization within and surrounding the community will expand on the rights of children. Finally, with the collaboration of these agencies, individuals, and organizations, basic services will be improved like education, health care, family unification, and feeding.

I have seen in African villages that need serious help. When the rainy seasons come, they will close the schools and community properties and leave their homes. Most hospitals are far away, and 95% of people don't have money to pay for their medication. People don't understand what the villages go through. There are more than 2 billion children out there who can't go to school because they don't have the opportunity. When they are sick, they don't go to hospitals, causing little illnesses to become life-threatening. All this happens because they don't have the support they need.

I wish that anyone who reads this book can open their heart to our siblings whose lives are taken from them thanks to poverty. I call upon your generosity and care towards them. I call upon your maximum generosity, kindness, care, mercy, love, and support to make a difference in others' lives and get the support I need to make my foundation into reality. Together we can make a difference in each other's lives and make the world a better place.

If we can give a little, then this unnecessary suffering will stop happening to these poorest people. I know that nothing comes easy and I'm willing to take any challenges, risks, tasks, and whatever it takes to make it happen. It's very sad and disappointing to see we live in a world where others must fight every day simply for food, clean water, and other basic needs. It breaks my heart to have to see that and see others experience that every day. That is why I wanted to share this with the world.

I know there are so many people out there who care and want to help, but they don't know-how. I also gain an understanding that in this world. I also realize that not everyone has their best intentions because there are so many bad people out there these days pretending they're helping those people in need while they're doing it for themselves. I needed to make the foundation into reality, but I'm still trying to reach out to people with my foundation website so that I can get the sponsorship I need to make my foundation dream come true. It's not just a dream; it's also personal for me and close to my heart.

Sometimes I wonder if others care deeply as I do for the poor children who are dying every day across the world. It's very sad and depressing to see those sweet children die because of poverty while others are here getting everything they want and still not appreciating what they have.

If we can all look back to our roots and look at the things our siblings are going through all over the world and try to act, that will be good because anyone can make a difference in those people's lives. I know it because I saw how my African brothers and sisters are living and every day the challenges they face to survive. All that comes with a price they must pay to stay alive, and every day any numbers of people die from poverty. Those people in need are like all of us, and they need someone to stand up for them and let them know that they're not alone. They're people out there who care about them, and they feel their pain, and everything will be okay.

If we can all think about those people, provide our helping hands, and show them that we care, that will be good because this life is too short, and people don't last forever. If we look after those people and help them rise from poverty and live in clean and healthy environments, have clean water to drink, good clothes to wear, good shelters to leave in, food to eat, opportunities to attend school, and be treated equally, they can start new lives and move on. I always wanted to contribute to change and to make our world a better place for the entire human race.

Sometimes I ask myself why others are ungrateful for what they have and why they don't help people who need it the most.

I believe there are good people out there who want to help, but they don't know-how. The HTIN 2010 foundation website is here to help people give back and fight for those people who can't fight for themselves together who can make a difference in those people's lives. My favorite artist, Michael Jackson said in his "heal the world" song, if you care about living make a little space to create a world a better place for the enter human race. I wish there were many more people like him in the world who would open their hearts to help others who can't stand for themselves.

If we can all look deep in our hearts and try to open little space there for all those people around the world who are suffering from poverty and diseases and join our helping hands together, we would not only give those people better lives but also make our world more beautiful.

I believe in the rights of everyone, and I believe that everyone should have their voice to say whatever they want to. Sometimes people tell me that I'm crazy, but the truth is I stand for what I believe in, and that is to fight for people who cannot fight or stand for themselves. For me, it means doing whatever it takes to make that happen and giving those people the voice and the support they need to stand for themselves by the grace of God.

Chapter 3

The importance of family and special people in your life

Ilearned another critical lesson is growing up, about the true meaning of family and close friends. Sometimes we do not think our families are important to us because we are growing up and we don't need our families anymore. But the truth is, we are wrong because we need our families in so many ways in our lives. Our families have our back when we are in trouble and during the bad and good times. Generally speaking, our families are the key to our success or achievements because they are there for us from the day, we're born to the day we die.

The first reason our families are prominent in our lives is that without the love and support of our families, we will not be who we are today or even think about following our dreams, achieving our goals, going to school, getting our dream job, dream house, and many more. Our families are our guides, anger, heroes. Our parents give up their lives to give us a better life and future and every parent's dream is to see their children have the best lives and futures they couldn't have. Parents do whatever it takes to see their children happy and have better lives even if it will cost them their whole lives.

Families are not something that you can buy at the market when you need it. It's a gift from God to us, but now we tend to forget the true meaning of family. We tend to create our definition of the family without using the essential values of the family until we get into trouble. We need to take family values very seriously because people don't last forever. I think that we all have to take a step back and think about the things our families had done for us and appreciate and honor them with everything we got before we forgot the people who make us who we are here because our families did everything they can to give us better lives they didn't have before.

Many people who don't have a family in their lives ask themselves what the value of family is. Some of those answers to those questions are something that no one can answer until they have their own families. I wish that we can realize and respect our families and be thankful to them every day of our lives.

Now is our turn to honor, support, appreciate, and be there for our families like they did for us. Now it is up to us to do the same for them, to protect and to take all their pains from them the way they did for us. But in our generation, we tend to think or say it's our parents' jobs to keep us safe and give us whatever we want, but the truth is that it's not. Our parents' choice to give up everything to give their children a better life and the sad and selfish thing about it is when we grow up, we don't thank them or appreciate them for that.

We all should think about why we became who we are today because that is significant. I think someday when we are prosperous; our first millions should go to the people we make that possible for us—our great families, the special people in our lives such as our true friends, and others who help us through our journey to get to where we are going.

We should think hard before we act because our actions affect our families. When we go through troubles or challenging times, they share it with us, and they stand by us all the way. We are to be true to ourselves and know our families are there for us to help us like how they were there for us. Since the day we were born, we have to also keep in mind that our true families are not there for us for our money or what we have, they're there for us to help us.

Because if we don't have loving and supportive families in our lives, we will not be completely individual or be able to do the things we enjoy, to follow our dreams and goals. The successful people I see have a family behind them to help them. I saw so many people who don't have any family in their lives that they wish they had some family in their lives, and they will do anything to get a family in their lives. It also helps me understand that it doesn't matter how rich or successful you are. If you don't have a family in your life, you would never be happy because our families are so much more than we think they are. That is how powerful the family is.

The family is something that money can't buy because the family is a creation from God. Also, realize that it doesn't matter if you are rich or poor. Mother Teresa said, "In this life, we cannot always do great things. But we can do small things with great love."

I want to tell all the teenagers out there not to take their parents for granted. They're critical people in our lives. I know sometimes we don't want to hear what our parents or families are telling us during our teenage years, but they're right. Our parents and family members try to help us be on the right track to reach our goals and dreams, but we don't like to hear their advice. We should take their advice seriously and more importantly, thank them for being there for us and helping us to be our future leaders and to achieve success.

Sometimes we don't know what we have until it's gone. Sometimes we don't see the bigger picture of life or what the future holds for us, but our families see it, and they try very hard to keep us on the right track. Through it all, our parents and families work so hard because they're our number one fans.

"The love of a family is life's greatest blessing."

—unknown

Because God creates us to have a family. Our families help us find our way back when we get lost and have a place to call home. Our true families and close friends are the only ones who can do that for us.

God created our parents and our families to be there for us. Our families are our circle of life, our hope, strength, love, and support. Our families are our world, everything because they're the ones who are there for us day and night to make sure we are ok and give us shoulders to cry on, someone to talk to when we want to talk. They give us a place to call home when we are lost or in trouble, because our families are also the special people in our lives and they're the best blessing and gift this life has to offer. Now families come in different sizes. Being a family with someone doesn't only mean people you share blood with. It also can mean devoted friends and other special people you have in your life who are there for you through tough times and good times too.

The true definition of family is people who can love others and treat others like their family; it doesn't have to be the same bloodline. Whatsoever but to have the courage to love others, help them during the difficult times in their lives to help them pass those times and also to have special people in your life to be proud to call a family; those are the true members of your family. The blessing of our parents is them giving up their dreams and goals so that we can achieve ours.

I also think it's vital we should think before we act because our actions affect not only us, but they also affect our loved ones as well because they feel our pains and sadness that are why we should about the things we do or actions.

We need to keep in mind that we know who our true families and close friends are because money or other things can make us lose the people that are especially important to us are our unique families and close friends.

We should not only use Mother's Day, Father's Day, birthdays, etc. to thank our parents and families. We should also use every day to show our appreciation to our parents, families, and others we are special to let to tell them how much we appreciate them. Because if you see, we are on this earth today is because of them, God makes them be our parents, families, and guarders to guard us to where our future holds for us. Our family and other essential people stand by us throughout our lives, and they see us when we are our worse, best, bad and sad they pick us down and wasp our tears and make us feel ourselves again our families and loved ones are the ones that do those things for us. They're there for us from day one until we become the person we want to become; our families are there along the way to help and support us.

And sometimes we tend to let our emotions take over our lives because of the feeling sometimes we tend to have toward some of our family members. We tend to think that everyone is going to hurt us, but we must let those feelings and memories go and know that those are our past and get over those things so that we can move on with our lives. No one is perfect, and we all make mistakes at some point in our lives but what matters is how to move on from there and live our past behind us that is what is essential in life and learn from those mistakes in the future. So that we don't repeat or make those mistakes again cause holding to those feelings and memories wouldn't do us any good it will keep us back to find our happiness and the value of family friendship.

I'm fortunate and thankful to have my cool family and close friends in my life. Those things and memories I have in my life are the things that help me get past every day of my life because without my family and close friends I wouldn't get through difficult times in my life. That is what the value of family and close friends did in my life, and I wish that people can take the benefits of family and close friends very seriously. Because the reason we are strong individuals is because of our family's love, support, and encouragement especially all of our wonderful mothers around the world for giving us the best gift of life. To all the mothers, fathers, family members, and loyal friends out there in the world, I say you all rock because all of you are the reason why we are the person we become today.

Chapter 4

Our self-image is an essential thing in a person's life

e true to yourself first before others. By knowing who you are and where you come from no matter how rich or important you are. Also never try to be something you are not, also never forget those who stood by you when you need them the most. Sometimes we don't know it, but every day of our lives we need people's help throughout the day, and how we present ourselves to others is very important. People see us as the person we are inside and outside because sometimes our actions, how we present ourselves can mislead others to think that that is who we are. That kind of misunderstanding can mess up our choice eventually.

Sometimes we tend to let our societies do our jobs for us, something that we should be doing for ourselves, we tend to let our societies make our height our true identities and harm us in our personal lives.

We are so much more than we think we are. If we let ourselves be and take risks, chances, we will see and discover what we are made of and what our abilities can do. We should not let others or things be afraid of showing who we are or our identity.

It's critical to know and keep in mind that anything is possible if we put our minds into it, we can be anything we want to. As well If we are willing to work hard and be true to ourselves, we can do whatever we want in life. If you do not change who you are, you will be surprised what you can do and what your abilities can do for you. It doesn't matter how hard your life is don't change our height your true identity from people around you because sometimes we don't see it, but our abilities are the creation of life and our future tomorrow that is why our self-respect, ourselves image, and our true identity is very important in our lives. If we are not true to ourselves, we will never be happy with ourselves until we know who we are, our true self, loyal to ourselves.

> "Be the change that you want to see in the world."

—Gandhi

The way we see ourselves also matters how we introduce ourselves to others. Our image and self-estate speak for themselves about the person we are, and the way others see us through those images, self-estate.

> "Trust yourself, create the kind of self that you will be happy to live with all your life."

—Golda Meir

Those quotes are trying to teach us about ourselves to be always loyal and true to ourselves and not trying to be somebody else because if you are not happy the way God created you, it doesn't matter what you have or what you become. You will never be happy with yourselves until you find yourself.

"You can't let other people tell you who you are. You have to decide that for yourself."

Always be yourself no matter what. The reason is if you can then you will be happy with yourself and be proud of who you are in life. That is the most rewarding gift this world has to offer. Be true and proud of yourself for who you are. And to fight for what is your own and never let anyone take that from you. Those are our tools in life because they are not something you buy, they're given to us by God, and you must fight hard and own it to get your self-respect.

Sometimes when you forget our true self, which is why we have our families and devoted friends to remind us of when we forget about who we are or where we came from when we are lost to help us find back our way back.

Every great successful person you see starts somewhere locally, honestly, are true to yourselves, challenging work, family, and close friends love and encourage those are the stories behind every successful people we see.

> "The time is always right to do what is right."
>
> —Martin Luther King Jr.

And believe in yourselves first before others will be because if you do not show people what you mean or who you are no one will, and you will be miserable in your life and people's mind.

People like us when we are ourselves but when we change to be somebody else or something we are not as hard to evening to find a friend or your loved ones to try to see you like another person who is not. We must guard the most important thing to us ourselves—respect. Most of the time we tend to be afraid to show who we truly are because of fearing people judging us or getting respect from others, but the truth is we are the ones that let people judge us.

God creates all of us in our ways to be ourselves; that is what makes all of us different inside and outside besides our skin colors, race, cultures, and language.

Our abilities are the way of life because they reflect to the world the kind of person we are. The problem is most of the time we don't realize what God has blessed us. The meaning of our true self and love ourselves.

In this world, we can live once, not two times. But what matters is we know who we are, our self-esteem and self-respect are critical for us to understand and value.

If we forgot who we are, it would be tough to become what we want to be in the future. How we introduce ourselves to the world, those are the things that people know us by and consider the kind of person who individually is. As well as what makes us unique individuals. Our positive attention or negative attention also can affect how people value and see us. We need to watch how we act or talk to others because sometimes we don't know how our actions or words affect others.

We have to try our best not to be offensive or drive people close to us away. We should make apologies to them because we are human, and everyone makes mistakes. What matters is how to do the right thing and fix those mistakes. We should not try to hide from the world or others because of how we look or define ourselves by our wealth or our skin color. We should know and be proud of the person we are besides all the things in ourselves and not be afraid of showing the world our arrogant self.

Another important thing is being honest, loyal, and true to yourself. In any aspect, it doesn't matter what life throws at you. If we are not honest, loyal, or true to ourselves, we would never be happy with ourselves.

We must embrace and be proud to show who we are because God brought us on this earth to make a mark in each other's lives. Be true to yourself because if not, time will run too fast. Reflecting on the past ten years or so, we will wish we never lost sight of ourselves. Life is too short.

Chapter 5

My journey through having a brain tumor

Being diagnosed with an atypical meningioma Grade 2 brain tumor was a wake-up call for me. It made me value life more than I used to and took every moment to count. In May of 2012, in just a few moments, everything changed in my life at the age of 21. The funny thing about is that. At first, I didn't think it was a big deal or something that almost took my life. I always think that I'm 100% healthy and I don't need to go to the hospital. That was a lesson for me to learn to take my health very seriously because you never know how everything will change in your life.

It all started during the exercise training I was doing. I fell and hit my head. The next thing I remember, they're telling me I got a concussion, but I didn't take it very seriously. But then the doctor ran more tests on my brain and told me that I have a brain tumor on the left side of my brain. From that moment, everything changed in my life.

I did so many MRIs, CT scans, and IVs, radiation therapy also drum any treatment drugs in my body. Also, the funny thing about it is that I never knew or even thought about a brain tumor until that day. The concussion was a good thing because we were able to catch the tumor before it spread to the rest of my brain. If I had left for training as planned without knowing that I had a brain tumor, I would not have survived to share my story with the world. I'm very thankful to be alive and enjoying the meaning of life.

Atypical meningioma Grade 2 brain tumor survivor.

A week or two after being diagnosed, I started having messy headaches, trouble sleeping, balancing, thinking, dizziness, mood changes. Also, at the time beginning stuffer some memory loss, to difficulty seeing clearly. I was also getting bad headaches five to six times a day and had problems concentrating. There was a lot of stuff was going through my body at that time. But I took everyday step by step with my family and friends. After all my options for different treatments to get well.

I still remember one of the treatments I hated was radiation therapy and taking medication, but I never entirely gave up each day I went through the same counties because I have a strong foundation of support around me cheering me up, gave me their encouragement to get through it each day to reach my goals of being free from this disaster call Atypical meningioma tumor. During my treatment, every day I come close to getting well with that strong mind sense of being finally free from the tumor. Now reflecting on my journey during my tumor, the setbacks I had, and each bad news about how my treatment was going make me feel too wanted to give up a few times but my loved ones wouldn't let me give up even thinking about it, they all went above and beyond with love and support to continue my fight against brain tumor and to win my battle as well.

Reflecting on my time fighting against brain tumors was one of another level milestone in my life that I would never forget because it was full of many dark days and nightmares that I have to endure from sometimes that feels like going through nightmares each with rounds of treatments, medications and uncontrollable noises in my head that were driving me crazy. To a point where a couple of times during my sickness, I questioned myself about why God is letting me go through all this pain after everything I had been through during my childhood. I even believed that God didn't love me. Also, the only light that keep me going and never forget about God was my beloved family and all my loved ones- the special people that had a significant impact on my life. But now looking back on my experiences and everything I have been through, I realize many things and learned many lessons along the way and one of those is God, the value of family which come in all form and still learning about things every day. Furthermore, one of the things I know 100 percent sure is that I was very wrong about God.

God never gave up, and he gave me the strength to fight for my life with the unconditional love, support, and encouragement of my number one fans, my mom, dad, siblings, and the rest of my family and friends. They're my heroes for not giving up on me before and now and helping me be alive today. I believe that this is all part of my destiny. During those times at the hospital other patients who I met there became friends. We used to tell each other what we are going through is not right cause people are enjoying their lives and having so much fun while we are at the hospital fighting for survival to stay alive. Now I know and learn another life lesson is that if I'm alive, there will be times when I must overcome the difficult times in my life.

Now looking back on my journal from a brain tumor I can't remember how many medications and different treatments that went through my system to get better. This year has been a hard year for me because of all the stuff I must go through to get well, but for some reason, I always get a second chance. At that moment I also felt like God, and the angels are looking over me to save me and be given another opportunity in so many ways. The best gift anyone can ask for is a healthy life, family, and close friends are the biggest gift of life is called love from God. Love gives us hope and faith gave us meaning and purpose in life. Being surviving a brain tumor and being given a second chance in life helped me value everything in life, even the ones I didn't before.

It was a significant transformation for me from healthy to being sick in a matter of days. When I was going through my journal, I experienced so many sad and stressful things get used to. I have met so many nice patients who have the tumor, cancer, and other stuff that was happening. Also during the process of recovery, I lose a couple of friends there who didn't make it alive was very stressful for me, and even get to hear others share their stories with me. Their journal, experiences it was heartbreaking but what help me and others who survive is that we have each other and our families and friends to get through it.

Every day wasn't easy, in many aspects, it was challenging for me to fight for my life to be alive, and is not easy for me, and the harder thing about it is that every day during my journey. Every time my doctor come to see me, I always got terrified because I didn't know if the doctor is going to tell me I have little time left. It's the only thing I think about when I see my doctor is the worst feeling ever. I remember when my doctor came to check on me, I still remember she kept telling me that I needed to stop thinking that I will never get well because my brain is not doing good, and my brain doesn't need more stress. But it's very hard not to stress because I don't know if I will survive and second is, I'm in the hospital where I see people die every day.

I can't thank my beautiful family and close friends for everything they all have done for me. My journey through having a tumor teaches me a lot about life and to value things that I have and to thank for so many things in my life. Now I want to become a brain surgeon someday because of my experiences and be a doctor like Aunt Miriam, to help people like my wonderful mom, sister, dad, and the rest of my awesome family and close friends.

I remember at the end of July my doctor came to check on me and that day was different from other days. I can still remember her looking at me with a joyful look. That day was going to bring my faith and hope for the future that I lost. Before I could tell her how I felt, she said to me, and I was getting better. That was the best news my doctor gave me since I got diagnosed and the first time, I knew my tumor was going away.

She said I was a brave and strong fighter and that my scans were improving. I remember telling her that I am not courageous or intense; it is my beautiful family and close friends who are the reason why I didn't stop fighting. At that moment, tears came to my eyes, and during those tough times, I never thought I would hear good news. I will survive the tumor or even want to share my story with my loved ones and with the world. I never think that from that moment was my past to recovery and be here today to want to help people who are going through the same or similar thing or others whose loved ones are going through. I know what it feels like to go through different obstacles and challenges at the same time that's why I wanted to share my story and personal experience with the world hopeful it can help others who are dealing and going through a similar thing to overcome those challenges and obstacles during those difficult times in their lives.

Now I know that there is a reason why I'm still alive, and for some reason, I got a second chance. It was a long journey for me from being healthy and outgoing to being diagnosed with the worst brain tumor ever when I didn't expect it, and I was going to be following my dreams and goals until my big, bigger nightmares came to life. When I got diagnosed, the first thing that came to my head was the tumor was going to kill me and no way was I going to survive it or get a second chance.

During my treatment, my Aunt Miriam, the doctor in NY, found me some sites to connect to others that are going through the same or similar things as me. I was going to get help and courage from each other through the site to win over our diseases and give each other hope to fight harder, and that site helped me out because we get to help each other and know how each other are doing every day. I made a lot of friends through the website who all know that I'm still fighting very hard, and I know one thing for so is that they were very sick too. Sharing our stories and experiences not only makes us feel better but also helps us try hard to stay alive and help each other get through it with our families and friends.

Caring Bridge gave me and the millions of patients who joined the site the will to stay strong and to push us to fight harder to get well. The site makes me look beyond my sickness and my pain to attempt to help others who are going through the same pains or similar ones and watch things from other people's points of view. I finally realized that love is more than what we think it is because during my tough times if I didn't have my family, friends, and those friends, I met during my journey, I wouldn't make it alive to today.

My second to the last journal that I posted in Caring Bridge let others know my status about how I was doing. It was about the good news I got from my doctor about my tumor. My doctor told me at the end of July that I'm getting well, and I also did with most of my treatments and medications and my chemo that was the coolest thing ever.

I couldn't believe that I'm finally free from the tumor; now I can move on with my life. I couldn't go through this challenging time of my life without the love and support of my wonderful mom, family, close friends, and other friends I met during my journal which helps me and pushes me to fight harder to get better. I'm very thankful to all of them from the bottom of my heart. There is nothing better about having people you love in your life there for you during tough times is a blessing for me to have such people like that in my life.

When diagnosed with an Atypical meningioma grade 2 brain tumor was the worst time of my life in so many ways. One of the difficult things I had to face during my journey was losing a family member and a couple of friends who were special to me. It was not an easy journey for me, but I survived it.

I always updated my status on how I was during in my brain tumor support group with the other patients for encouragement such as how I was doing and feel like remembering the time I post in my support group each day during my journey to when I was free from a brain tumor, for example, one of my posts after the tumor was this "(Ever since I got free from the tumor, almost one month now, I feel so much better than I did before and have a primary focus and strength of my life to this moment. I have been very blessed with another gift of life, which is the chance of being a life again for the second time in my life and at this time I will use every moment and opportunity to count and worthwhile and do all the things I wanted to do I didn't do before. I will work harder than before to achieve all my dreams, goals, and passions)" because I kept a notebook during my tumor journey to write down how I was feeling daily and afterward I posted some of the does on my support group page.

After surviving a brain tumor, I had so many things to be thankful for also I'm still fortunate in so many ways, and I'm very thankful for God, my family, close friends, and the special gift of life that I got. I never thought I would survive or be free from the tumor or be home now finishing my recovery and finishing my book.

Now I have this opportunity to tell my story with my loved ones and also with the world, I have so much to be thankful for especial my great mom, dad, big sister, and the rest of my family and wonderful friends from childhood friends, to the close friends I have now all of who help me so much.

Now I'm very proud of sharing my journey through having a tumor with the world to help others deal with the same or similar things. I can finally be happy and proud to share my story with my loved ones and the world as well. The crazy thing is that I can't return to school in August of 2013 due to my brain. I must get a full recovery and finish my treatment. I wanted to go to school very badly because I was very tired of staying home bored and completing my restoration. After two years of treatment and recovery, the only thing I can do at that time is to work on my book and take more medications every day. I hated that very much taking one drug to the other, and I miss school a lot that time, but I have to leave school thing for later when my brain gets a full recovery, now my brain is doing very well. Then I started to regain all my memories back, and I thank god, all my loved ones for that special my mom and big sister and all the special people in my life. Who stands by me and helps me go through this journey, it's a big blessing for me to have all the great people I have in my life from families to friends and I'm forever grateful for that.

The day I left the hospital at the end of August 2012, the first thing I did was listen to some of my voicemails on my phone that and my big sock and disappointment was listing to those voice messages it makes me sad. The funny thing about it is listening to those messages on my phone it doesn't only make me upset and also more stressed after listing to those messages. I knew right from a moment people who care about and who don't because sometimes you don't know who cares about you or your true friends are until you go through hard times.

It felt hurt to hear those messages that I heard on my phone after being in the hospital for a long time, and that was not the welcome back I was hoping to hear from people that I care about and considered my friends. I'm very hurt by those people to leave me those messages while I was fighting very hard to survive and was between life and death moment the time those messages were left on my phone. It came as a surprise to me.

I wish that they had thought a moment before sending me those messages because I didn't know what was going through in my life during those times, they sent me that voice mail cause that was the last thing I needed. I wouldn't quote those messages because they make me upset. I wish that people could think first and watch what they said to others or do because our action affects others around us.

I always try very hard every day of my life to be kind and respectful to others, that is how I was brought up, and the voicemails that I got from those people was not what I was hoping to get that same thing and return, to be treated with kindness and respect the same thing I show others.

I would never forget those words they said in my voicemails from the side with me to the rest of my life and I would always remember those horrible messages got the day I left the hospital after my long journey from the tumor.

Sometimes it doesn't matter how much you think you know someone they tend to surprise you in a way when you are not expecting it. That is what happens to me. I think I know someone, but the truth is I don't know. I don't know why I got diagnosed with a brain tumor. I don't have the answers for that what I do know is everything happens for a reason. I'm still alive, and I got another second chance in life, to make every second count and to turn some part of my life for the better and also to get the chance to able to do the things I wanted to do before I got sick.

I'm well now and out of the hospital and thanks to all of them for helping me through the difficult times. I can try to pick my life up soon where I left off. Now I have so much more to live for and the ability to do things differently and change some part of my life around me. I had something that not everyone gets to have a second chance God gave me to believe in myself and not to care about what others said or think about me. Being sick made me realize many things that I did not take into account or consider were important, and I should take them into account.

Now I look back on my journey from one treatment to another with chemo and all the stuff that went through in my system to get well and be myself again. Looking at those horrifying moments in my life was something that I would never forget or take for useless. All those pains and stuffing I went through now are natural for me to talk about it than before when I was going through it.

And all those times my family and close friends never left me for a second they're all being by my side through life, I'm thankful because I couldn't do anything with my incredible family and close friends for standing by myself along the way loving and supporting me.

I can never pay them back enough for everything they have done for me since the day I arrive on this earth, but I will always remember everything they all have done for the honor of love, support, joy, strength, and courage they have given me. It's a blessing for me not only the surviving tumor but all the people I have in my life to get this opportunity to share my story and others who are not here today to share their own stories to help others who are facing the same or similar things too.

God, my sweet family, close friends, and the friends I met during my journey are the reason I 'm alive today, have the strength and courage to bite my tumor. It also gave me another lesson to learn that I should face my worst fears and overcome my bad nightmares to take control of my life, don't let any sickness or thing take over my life.

It was an unbelievable gift of life is surviving I remember when I was sick, the only thing running to my mind was wealth I will never survive, or am I going to get well and be myself again those experiences. I gained during my journal is something that I wouldn't trade for anything cause the experiences and journal will be my voice and others who didn't make it today to help others around the world who are going through. The same or similar things to support them past those difficult times so that someday I can also use those experiences to be the voice of others too.

When my doctors cleared me on October 3, I left Alaska for New York where I'm living with my sister to finish my recovery so that my brain can get back to normal so that I can return to school. I can't believe it when my doctor told me that I was clear to fly. It reminds me of the day she first said to me that I would be ok, and I would get well soon. I never thought I would ever hear those things or even be alive today. It's incredible how far I have come from being hospitalized and fighting for my life, all the pain, memory loss, and blackouts.

Sometimes it's funny how life is because if someone asked me when diagnosed that I will be alive today and to finish my book today, I wouldn't believe it at that time and even be here in NY living with my sister today. Now I'm walking on my legs with not holding anything to be able to walk all my wildest imagination I didn't think I would see this day or be here finishing my book right now.

I'm forever thankful for my life. I have everything in life I ever wanted. I have God in my life, the best mom, dad, big sister, brothers, sisters, uncles, aunts, grandparents, and other family members who stood by me all my life. As well to be giving the best gift of life is true friendships that all m friends have given me. They're not only my true friends but also my loyal and honest friends. Who are not just special friends to me but also a family to me from my childhood friends to all the wonderful friends I got here in the U.S from my Bartlett family to my UAA family to other special friends?

Being told I have a brain tumor was one of the best things ever to happen to me because it makes me value life and people that are in my life more and special thanks to my parents for beginning me into this earth and all my siblings for having me as their sister with unconditional love and support they gave me over the years and continue to give me each day. Also furthermore has well to all my grandparents, uncles, aunts, and my other family members who I don't name, thank you for loving, supporting, encouraging, and other stuff they all have, giving me to win against my tumor. I wouldn't have the courage and strength to fight harder to survive if it wasn't for them. Also, they have made me the person I am today, an Atypical meningioma Grade 2 brain tumor survivor.

Chapter 6

Our goals and dreams

Our dreams are significant to us because they're the creation of life without our dreams or goals that we bring to life, our world will be a mess-up, and our societies wouldn't be the way it's today. Our dreams are what make us human beings because God gave us opportunities to dream and turn those dreams into reality and no dream is too small to achieve and to achieve those dreams we have. At the same time we also have to believe in them and be willing to work hard to follow our dreams wherever they make lead us in life that is what differentiates us from other living things for example animals also have dreams, but they don't have that opportunity like we did to bring their goals into reality.

Someone once told me if you want to be successful in life, you must be willing to work extremely hard and take everything as a challenge to you. Don't look back; always move forward. That is why we have our dreams and goals to guard us through our density. ("Dr. John F. DeMartini once said in a quote, "When you follow the dream in your heart, you're energized, inspired, & motivated.")

Because our dreams are beyond ourselves, and sometimes we don't see or know it, but there and it doesn't matter who we aren't or where we came from. Also, it's vital to put those dreams into play and make something big, useful than we imagine and use those dreams we have to help and care for others and also use every moment count without not waste. We need to use those dreams we have to make a difference and influence each other in a good way instant of destroying each other because our dreams are the wisdom of life and the persuasive skills, we all must create a better world for our future children and grandchildren.

Sometimes we tend to think we are not smart enough or good enough to achieve our dreams and goals, but the truth is we can accomplish anything if we believe we can do whatever we want to if we let our dreams lead us to where we are going.

We also could make our dreams something biggest not only for ourselves but for others around us to make difference in their lives with our dreams and the goals we individuals have for ourselves to help us to make our lives meaningful and joyful that is the reason we have our dreams. We are what we make of our dreams because our dreams and goals are the creation of life and it's what we make of our dreams and goals not only for our happiness but also for the environments we live in. The goals we set for ourselves with our dreams help us overcome our fears and challenge ourselves in the things that look like they can't do or the impossible things.

Some don't believe in themselves or don't know what we can do with our dreams or turn them to until we believe in our dreams and goals. If we don't have dreams or goals, we wouldn't be able to be doctors, nurses, lawyers, teachers, military personnel, firefighters, police officers, and so many more all of that because of ourselves; if we don't have ourselves, it would be hard for us to achieve all of that.

Most of the time things we dream of are more significant than ourselves, but that doesn't mean that we should give up on our dreams or the goals we set for ourselves. Because anything is possible if we believe and have faith that we can do it because our dreams are so much more and are the gift god create us with is our talents and our creation in this world.

Our dreams help us challenge ourselves to the best of our abilities and also help us to discover our true self what we are mead of, but it doesn't come quickly to achieve most of our dreams. In able to fulfill many of our dreams and goals requires t education and college degrees and hard work these days to accomplish whatever dreams or goals we have.

Our goals are the map that leads us to our future and tomorrow's leader that helps us find our density in life and to help us to get through the long journey we all have ahead of us. And our dreams are our wisdom of life because our dreams lead us to the future and the person, we each want to become tomorrow, and our dream is our key to the future.

We should never let our fears get in the way or hold us back from achieving our dreams and goals in life or the person we want to be. Our goals motivate us to make our dreams by believing in ourselves to get to where our dreams take us.

> "I know where I'm going, and I know the truth, and I don't have to be what you want me to be. I'm free to be what I want."

> —Muhammad Ali

Those are some of the examples of why we should have faith and believe in ourselves to follow our dreams not somebody else and be true to ourselves always because our dreams are more prominent than we think if we let ourselves dream more.

We must follow our dreams and goals to where they lead us and have in store for us. Sometimes we tend to think or want our dreams to happen for us overnight, but that is not the case all the time. Also to achieve our dreams and goals we have to be willing to work hard even with that we can do anything we put our minds into and not make excess. That we are not smart or don't have what it take to achieve our dreams or goals because we can if they're important to us we will find a way to reach those dreams and goals we have doesn't matter how difficult those dreams or goals are are for us to succeed.

> "If you don't have a dream, how are you going to make a dream come true."

> —Oscar Hammerstein

Without our dreams or goals, we wouldn't be the things we want to be or become or get all the successes in the world and hard work too.

Our dreams and goals open the doors for us in the future because our dreams are the visions for tomorrow. Our dreams are the light to see what the future holds for us and make us keep dreaming bigger and not stop dreaming or setting goals for ourselves. And it also helps us answer these questions we have or might have what dreams are? The dream is on the road to our future, and even our dream is the motivation that leads us to wherever our goals might take us tomorrow.

Our dreams and goals are our tools on this earth, and we should let our dreams take us to where our dreams need to guide us. Our dreams define who we are and what we become tomorrow, and our dreams and goals help us to bring our creation to life. Our dreams are tomorrow's future because they're the doors to what tomorrow holds for us.

Sometimes we don't realize what our dreams and goals can do or lead us to until we believe, have faith, and work hard. And even every dream we have has its challenge to achieve it, but hard work and education achieve any hard dreams or goals because knowledge is an essential thing in life even to get to where you are going or accomplish any task, dream, or goal. Because if we don't have higher education these days it would be tough to make our dreams or goals and I wouldn't say it would be impossible, but it would be tough to accomplish because without education it would be hard to make our dreams or goals or evenly get our dream jobs.

And sometimes we tend to forget our dreams and follow our friend's dreams because we tend to think our dreams are more comfortable and possible to achieve. However, also those kinds of things are wrong because no dream is too small or impossible. After all, we can accomplish any goals we want if we put our minds to them and bring those dreams into reality.

John F. Kennedy once quoted, "We need men who can dream of things that never were." Because if we can't dream and believe in ourselves to follow our dreams, we will never achieve them.

Most of the time we get afraid to follow and achieve our dreams and goals because of the fear we have that we are not smart enough or don't have high enough education to make those dreams and goals, but the truth is we can accomplish any dreams or goals if we want to or believe.

Also, our dreams and goals help us to find our true self and the meaning of our dreams, goals. Because if we don't let ourselves dream and bring those dreams into reality, our world will be mess-up because our dreams are full of creation and wisdom of life that is, why we have that opportunity to dream and bring those dreams into reality than another living thing. When we dreams and set goals for ourselves, we are not only creating a better world but also making a difference in each other's lives with those dreams and goals in our lives. We need to have faith and follow our dreams wherever they will lead us tomorrow because whenever we dream or have goals and turn those dreams into reality, we can bring so much joy in this world and be whoever we want to be or achieve anything in life.

However, sometimes we tend to think that some of our dreams or goals are small and they're useless to follow because those small dreams or goals would waste our dreams To become the person who wants to be in the future but the truth is no dream or goal is too short of achieving or useless we have to stop thinking like that because that kind of thinking tends to kill our spirits of believing on our dreams and goals to even want to dream big.

We need to continue dreaming big for our children and our grandchildren because if we don't believe in ourselves and our dreams, it would be hard to help others to follow their dreams. Each dream we make if we pursue and achieve them and put them into play would make a difference in both our lives and others as well.

Our dreams are our imagination but what matters is what we do with them and what we make of them is what matters because if we don't know what to do with our dreams. It would be tough to understand what our dreams and goals will lead us or what our dreams have in store for us in the future. There's nothing that can't do; it just takes hard work, faith, and belief to make things happen even in small or big dreams. It can be achieved if we believe because we wouldn't know what our dreams have planned for us in the future until we put those dreams and goals into reality and see what they can do for us.

It's critical to believe in our dreams, goals because it's what helps us lead to our destiny. Our dreams and goals matter in our lives because our dreams and goals make us challenge ourselves and work hard to find our true self and what we are in this world to do. That is why we have our dreams and goals—to help us discover why we dream to help us achieve our life goals to get to where we are going and be the person we wanted to be for ourselves.

Chapter 7

Achievement and success

The five necessary steps to achieve success is challenging work, taking risks, performing tasks, taking challenges, having faith, and believing in yourself. Those are the steps to achieving success because, without those steps, we each wouldn't be successful individuals today. Because achievement and success don't come easy, you must be willing to work hard and own it to be successful because to be able to achieve something even is in school, workplace, or our personal lives, and you must be willing to give your whole heart and soul into it.

Success doesn't happen overnight; it takes time, a lot of challenging work, and many failures before achieving success and achievement because failure comes before achieving success, and every successful person we see starts from somewhere, failing along the way. But in today's generation, the mistakes we make mean we become afraid of taking chances. We shouldn't give up our dreams or the things we love because of being fearful of taking chances and having failures.

Success and achievement are not something that you get free or easy. It's something that you must own and work very hard to understand.

> "Achievement seems to relate to action. Successful men and women keep moving. They make mistakes, but they don't quit."
>
> —Conrad Hilton

Success comes with a lot of responsibility; that is why failures prepare us and challenge us to be successful and good leaders in our communities and future leaders of tomorrow.

> "If your success is not on your terms, if it looks good to the world but does not feel good in your heart, it is not a success at all."
>
> —Anna Quindell

Because of your success, you must be willing to take risks and challenge yourself more than your fellow students, co-workers, and many more. In many aspects it's essential to take o consideration before you become successful, you have to face so many ups and downs and see many failures along the way. To be a successful person, you must be willing to overcome anything life throws at you because every great success and achievement comes with hard work and challenges.

However, in some cases, success is not the only important thing in our lives. We tend to think because they're more important things than success such as family, friends, dreams, goals, passion, and the values we all leave and standby in our lives. And success comes in different ways, good or bad, and if we can know that life is more than success, then the world will be much better than it is now.

Because to be successful you must overcome your worst fears and go after what you love and enjoy doing with all your heart and soul into it with challenging work. The failures we have along the way to achieve success are the lessons for us to be reasonable people that are not afraid of anything.

"Success is a state of mind. If you want success, start thinking of yourself as a success."

—Dr. Joyce Brothers

Because if you don't believe you can achieve success, then no one will. In able to accomplish a successful outcome, you need a lot of help and guidance because you need connections to get success and achievement these days and to push you harder. What we don't know is our abilities can not only help us achieve success but so much more and also to expires failures when it comes to us and whatever we do we should put our heart and sold to become successful and achievement at our ways if we let ourselves be without not be afraid of failures.

We shouldn't let success come to us to be successful we should go to it and had very to gain our success and achievement with hard work because we can't own success without working very hard for It. Being successful and an achiever means how to be a reasonable, hard worker, not being afraid of taking calculated risks and chances also the same time following all the critical steps needed to overcome whatever challenges that come your way. To achieve success because before success and achievement failure comes first also can accomplish any degree of success, you first have to accept failures. Even to know what it takes to become an achiever or successful individual at whatever job duties or position we all do that is what achievement and success are all about willing to work very hard, belief in ourselves, challenge ourselves in all we do that is what success and accomplishment are all about in many aspects.

However, sometimes we tend to think that success and achievement are easy to get. Most of the time we tend to believe that we have to win and achieve success in everything without considering a failure that helped us challenge ourselves to go above and beyond our expectation to improve also achieve greatness because without any failure along the way we wouldn't get to where we are going in general. We have to own our success and achievement in ourselves and try to give it our all in everything we do. Hard work is what turns our world around and makes it a better place for ourselves and also to own things we want in life such as being successful people now or in the future and also recognized for our hard work or abilities those are the way to own achievement and success.

However, the value of being successful and an achiever is taking a risk and conquering whatever challenges come your way, and turning them into positive things that are what success and achievement are all about because those things to remember we wouldn't know or gain a funny understanding what success and achievement mean in general. Use those abilities to convert it to something bigger or to get recognized for your hard work. Most of the time we don't get recognized for our hard work, but that shouldn't let us give up on the things we love. We all can achieve success and achievement to be willing to accept failures, challenges, and whatever risks it brings along to become successful and to gain great accomplishment all of that comes from challenging work. Most of the time we get scared of taking a chance or challenges because of challenging work; therefore it's not as bad as it sounds.

And, be willing to do whatever is a necessity to be successful or get recognized for our hard work without cheating, through hard work, taking risks—those are the way to achieve success and the key to everything in life because hard work can help you made whatever you want in life.

www.ingramcontent.com/pod-product-compliance
Lightning Source LLC
Chambersburg PA
CBHW031232120626
46545CB00003B/1101